Chapter 1: The New Age of Business

The Evolution of Business Models

The evolution of business models has undergone significant transformations over the past few decades, driven by technological advancements, changing consumer preferences, and a growing emphasis on sustainability. Traditional business models, which relied heavily on linear production processes and consumerism, are being challenged by new paradigms that prioritize ethical practices and environmental responsibility. The shift towards sustainable business practices has led organizations to rethink their strategies, focusing on long-term value creation rather than short-term profits. This change is not merely a trend; it reflects a fundamental reorientation towards a more responsible approach to business.

Digital transformation plays a crucial role in shaping the future of business models. With the rise of digital technologies, companies are increasingly leveraging data analytics, artificial intelligence, and cloud computing to enhance operational efficiency and customer engagement. These tools enable businesses to create more personalized experiences, streamline processes, and innovate rapidly. As organizations adapt to this digital landscape, they are discovering new ways to deliver value to customers while minimizing their environmental footprint. This transformation is not just about technology; it requires a shift in mindset that embraces agility, collaboration, and continuous improvement.

Remote work innovations have also significantly influenced business models, particularly in the wake of the global pandemic. The traditional office-centric model has evolved into flexible arrangements that prioritize employee well-being and productivity. Companies are now exploring hybrid models that combine remote and in-person work, enabling them to attract diverse talent from various geographical locations. This shift not only enhances the work-life balance for employees but also reduces overhead costs and environmental impact. As organizations embrace remote work, they are redefining their operational structures and fostering a culture that values trust, autonomy, and results.

The integration of artificial intelligence into business strategies is reshaping how companies operate and interact with their stakeholders. AI technologies are being utilized to automate processes, improve decision-making, and enhance customer experiences. From chatbots that provide 24/7 support to predictive analytics that inform product development, AI is driving efficiency and innovation across industries. As businesses harness the power of AI, they must also consider ethical implications, ensuring that these technologies are used responsibly and inclusively. This approach fosters trust and transparency, essential components for building lasting relationships with customers and communities.

Social entrepreneurship and circular economy models are gaining traction as businesses recognize the importance of purpose-driven initiatives. Entrepreneurs are increasingly focusing on creating social impact alongside financial returns, addressing pressing societal challenges through innovative solutions. Circular economy models, which emphasize resource efficiency and waste reduction, are transforming how products are designed, produced, and consumed. By prioritizing sustainability, businesses can not only contribute to environmental preservation but also enhance their competitiveness in a market that values ethical practices. As these trends continue to evolve, businesses that embrace innovative models will be well-positioned to thrive in tomorrow's economy.

Key Trends Shaping Tomorrow's Marketplace

The marketplace of tomorrow is being reshaped by several key trends that reflect the evolving needs and values of consumers and businesses alike. One significant trend is the shift towards sustainable business practices. As awareness of climate change and environmental degradation grows, businesses are increasingly adopting eco-friendly strategies. This includes reducing waste, utilizing renewable resources, and implementing sustainable supply chains. Companies that prioritize sustainability not only improve their environmental impact but also attract a growing base of environmentally conscious consumers who prefer brands that align with their values.

Digital transformation strategies are another pivotal factor influencing the future marketplace. The rapid advancement of technology has created an imperative for businesses to embrace digital tools and platforms. From e-commerce to cloud computing, companies that leverage digital solutions can enhance operational efficiency, improve customer engagement, and gain a competitive edge. As more businesses move towards online models, the integration of digital technologies becomes essential for staying relevant and meeting the evolving expectations of consumers who increasingly favor convenience and accessibility.

Remote work innovations are reshaping the traditional workplace, leading to a shift in organizational structures and employee dynamics. The pandemic has accelerated the adoption of remote work, and many businesses are rethinking their approach to workforce management. Flexible work arrangements not only enhance employee satisfaction and productivity but also allow companies to tap into a broader talent pool. As remote work becomes a permanent fixture for many organizations, fostering strong virtual collaboration and communication will be crucial to maintaining a cohesive company culture.

Artificial intelligence is playing a transformative role in business operations, driving efficiencies and enabling data-driven decision-making. AI applications are being utilized across various sectors, from automating routine tasks to enhancing customer service through chatbots and personalized recommendations. This technology not only streamlines processes but also empowers businesses to analyze consumer behavior and market trends more effectively. As AI continues to evolve, its integration into business strategies will be vital for companies looking to innovate and remain competitive in an increasingly complex marketplace.

Lastly, the emphasis on wellness and mental health in the workplace is gaining traction as organizations recognize the importance of employee well-being. Businesses are implementing initiatives that support mental health, promote work-life balance, and foster inclusive environments. This focus on holistic employee wellness is proving to enhance productivity, reduce turnover, and improve overall workplace morale. As companies strive to create healthier and more inclusive work environments, they will be better positioned to attract and retain top talent, ultimately driving success in the marketplace of tomorrow.

The Role of Innovation in Business Evolution

Innovation serves as the cornerstone of business evolution, driving organizations to adapt and thrive in an ever-changing landscape. As we navigate through the complexities of the 21st century, businesses face unprecedented challenges and opportunities. The integration of new technologies, shifting consumer expectations, and the pressing need for sustainable practices compel companies to rethink their strategies. By fostering a culture of innovation, businesses can not only enhance their competitive edge but also contribute positively to society and the environment, paving the way for a sustainable future.

Sustainable business practices are now more critical than ever, as consumers and stakeholders demand accountability and transparency. Innovation in this realm involves reimagining products, services, and supply chains to minimize environmental impact while maximizing value. Companies are increasingly adopting circular economy models, which prioritize resource efficiency and waste reduction. By embracing innovative approaches to sustainability, businesses can create new revenue streams, improve brand loyalty, and ensure compliance with evolving regulations, all while contributing to a healthier planet.

Digital transformation strategies are another vital aspect of innovation in business evolution. As organizations digitize their operations, they unlock new efficiencies and enhance customer experiences. The adoption of artificial intelligence plays a crucial role in this transformation, enabling businesses to leverage data analytics for improved decision-making and personalized offerings. By integrating AI into their processes, companies can automate routine tasks, gain insights into consumer behavior, and enhance operational efficiency, leading to a more agile and responsive business model.

Remote work innovations have emerged as a significant trend, reshaping the traditional workplace. The COVID-19 pandemic accelerated the adoption of remote work, prompting organizations to explore new tools and technologies that facilitate collaboration and productivity. This shift has not only transformed work-life balance but also encouraged a more inclusive approach to talent acquisition, allowing companies to tap into a diverse global workforce. As remote work continues to evolve, businesses must innovate continually to maintain employee engagement and well-being while ensuring organizational cohesion.

Lastly, customer experience enhancement is a critical area where innovation can drive business success. In a world saturated with choices, companies must differentiate themselves by creating memorable and personalized experiences for their customers. Utilizing emerging technologies such as blockchain can enhance transparency and trust, while also providing secure transactions and improved supply chain management. By prioritizing customer-centric innovation, businesses can foster loyalty, drive growth, and ultimately contribute to a more sustainable future. In this dynamic environment, those who embrace innovation will not only survive but thrive, shaping the future of business for generations to come.

Chapter 2: Sustainable Business Practices

Defining Sustainability in Business

Sustainability in business is a multifaceted concept that extends beyond mere environmental considerations. It encompasses a holistic approach that integrates economic viability, social equity, and environmental stewardship. At its core, sustainability in business is about creating long-term value for all stakeholders, including customers, employees, suppliers, and the wider community. This definition challenges traditional business models that prioritize short-term profits over sustainable practices, urging organizations to adopt strategies that contribute positively to society and the planet.

The importance of sustainability in the business landscape has been amplified by growing consumer awareness and regulatory pressures. Today's consumers are increasingly making purchasing decisions based on a company's commitment to sustainable practices. Businesses that proactively embrace sustainability can distinguish themselves in a crowded marketplace, fostering loyalty and enhancing brand reputation. This shift is not merely a trend; it reflects a fundamental change in consumer expectations, where ethical considerations and environmental impact are integral to the decision-making process.

Incorporating sustainability into business strategies involves a comprehensive approach that includes social entrepreneurship, diversity, and inclusion initiatives. Organizations are recognizing that a diverse and inclusive workforce not only drives innovation but also aligns with the principles of sustainability by reflecting the communities they serve. By prioritizing social equity and engaging in fair labor practices, businesses can cultivate a positive workplace culture that promotes well-being and mental health, ultimately boosting employee productivity and satisfaction.

The advent of digital transformation and technologies such as artificial intelligence and blockchain plays a crucial role in advancing sustainability. These innovations enable businesses to optimize their operations, reduce waste, and improve transparency in supply chains. For instance, blockchain technology can enhance traceability, allowing companies to verify the sustainability of their sourcing practices. Furthermore, digital tools facilitate remote work innovations, reducing the carbon footprint associated with commuting and office space usage, thus contributing to a more sustainable operational model.

Lastly, the concept of a circular economy is pivotal in redefining business sustainability. This model encourages businesses to rethink traditional linear approaches—take, make, dispose—by promoting resource efficiency and waste reduction. Companies are increasingly adopting circular practices, such as recycling and repurposing materials, to minimize environmental impact. By prioritizing sustainability, businesses can not only address pressing global challenges but also unlock new opportunities for innovation and growth, ensuring their relevance in tomorrow's evolving economic landscape.

Implementing Sustainable Supply Chains

Implementing sustainable supply chains has become a critical focus for businesses aiming to thrive in the modern economy. As organizations increasingly recognize the importance of environmental responsibility and social equity, they are integrating sustainability into every aspect of their supply chain management. This involves re-evaluating sourcing, production, distribution, and disposal processes to minimize environmental impact and enhance social value. By adopting sustainable practices, companies not only contribute to a healthier planet but also improve their brand reputation, attract conscientious consumers, and realize cost efficiencies over time.

A sustainable supply chain begins with responsible sourcing. Businesses must prioritize suppliers who adhere to ethical labor practices, use environmentally friendly materials, and demonstrate a commitment to reducing their carbon footprint. This can involve establishing partnerships with local producers to support regional economies while minimizing transportation emissions. By investing in sustainable sourcing strategies, companies can ensure that their supply chain aligns with their values and resonates with consumers who are increasingly making purchase decisions based on ethical considerations.

Digital transformation plays a pivotal role in implementing sustainable supply chains. By leveraging advanced technologies, companies can gain real-time insights into their supply chain operations, allowing them to identify inefficiencies and areas for improvement. For instance, data analytics can help businesses track resource consumption, waste generation, and carbon emissions throughout their supply chain. This information can be used to optimize logistics, reduce waste, and implement circular economy models where products are reused, refurbished, or recycled, thereby extending their lifecycle and minimizing environmental impact.

Artificial intelligence (AI) and blockchain technologies are also transforming the landscape of sustainable supply chains. AI can enhance decision-making processes by predicting demand patterns and optimizing inventory levels, leading to reduced overproduction and waste. Meanwhile, blockchain offers unprecedented transparency, enabling companies to trace the origin of materials and verify supplier practices. This not only fosters trust among consumers but also ensures compliance with sustainability standards, creating a more accountable and resilient supply chain.

Lastly, fostering a culture of wellness and inclusion within organizations is essential for the successful implementation of sustainable supply chains. As businesses adopt new practices and technologies, they must also prioritize the mental health and well-being of their workforce. Managers should encourage collaboration and innovation, creating an environment where employees feel valued and empowered to contribute to sustainability initiatives. By embracing diversity and inclusion, organizations can tap into a wider range of perspectives and ideas, ultimately driving more effective and sustainable solutions. In this way, implementing sustainable supply chains not only benefits the environment and society but also enhances overall business performance.

Measuring and Reporting Sustainability Efforts

Measuring and reporting sustainability efforts is essential for businesses aiming to thrive in an increasingly eco-conscious marketplace. Organizations must establish robust frameworks to track their environmental, social, and governance (ESG) performance. This involves identifying key performance indicators (KPIs) relevant to sustainability goals, such as carbon footprint reduction, waste management efficiency, and social impact metrics. By systematically measuring these KPIs, companies can pinpoint areas for improvement, allocate resources effectively, and demonstrate accountability to stakeholders.

Incorporating technology plays a crucial role in enhancing the measurement and reporting of sustainability efforts. Digital transformation tools, including data analytics platforms and sustainability software, enable organizations to gather real-time data on their operations. These technologies facilitate the tracking of resource usage and emissions, allowing businesses to make informed decisions. Moreover, artificial intelligence can analyze vast amounts of data to identify patterns and predict future impacts, empowering organizations to adapt their strategies proactively.

Transparency in reporting is vital to building trust with consumers, investors, and other stakeholders. Businesses should adopt standardized reporting frameworks, such as the Global Reporting Initiative (GRI) or the Sustainability Accounting Standards Board (SASB), to ensure consistency and comparability in their disclosures. By openly sharing their sustainability performance, challenges, and strategies, organizations can foster a culture of accountability and demonstrate their commitment to sustainable practices.

Engaging stakeholders in the process of measuring and reporting sustainability efforts is equally important. Companies should actively involve employees, customers, and community members in discussions related to sustainability goals and achievements. This engagement not only enhances the credibility of the reports but also encourages a sense of ownership and responsibility among stakeholders. By incorporating diverse perspectives, businesses can uncover innovative solutions and strengthen their sustainability initiatives.

Lastly, integrating sustainability reporting into the core business strategy can drive long-term success. Organizations that prioritize sustainability are more likely to attract customers who value ethical practices, leading to increased brand loyalty and market competitiveness. Furthermore, as regulations around sustainability reporting become more stringent, businesses that proactively measure and report their efforts will be better positioned to comply with legal requirements. Ultimately, a commitment to transparency in sustainability practices not only enhances corporate reputation but also paves the way for a sustainable future.

Chapter 3: Digital Transformation Strategies

Understanding Digital Transformation

Digital transformation represents a fundamental shift in how organizations operate and deliver value to their customers. It encompasses the integration of digital technology into all areas of a business, fundamentally changing how the business functions and how it interacts with its stakeholders. This transformation is not merely about adopting new technologies; it requires a cultural change that challenges the status quo and encourages organizations to experiment, adapt, and innovate continuously. As businesses navigate this new landscape, understanding the principles of digital transformation becomes crucial for ensuring long-term sustainability and competitiveness.

At the core of digital transformation lies the need for businesses to leverage data effectively. Data-driven decision-making enables organizations to gain insights into customer behaviors, market trends, and operational efficiencies. By harnessing big data analytics, businesses can tailor their offerings to meet customer needs more precisely, thus enhancing customer experience. Moreover, the ability to analyze vast amounts of data in real-time allows companies to respond swiftly to changing market dynamics, ensuring they remain relevant and agile in an increasingly competitive environment.

Artificial intelligence (AI) plays a pivotal role in driving digital transformation across various sectors. From automating routine tasks to providing predictive analytics, AI enhances operational efficiency and fosters innovation. Businesses can utilize AI to streamline processes, reduce costs, and improve decision-making. For instance, AI-powered chatbots can enhance customer service by providing instant responses to inquiries, while machine learning algorithms can identify patterns and trends that inform strategic planning. Embracing AI not only drives productivity but also positions organizations to explore new business models and revenue streams.

The rise of remote work innovations is another significant aspect of digital transformation. As the workforce becomes more dispersed, businesses must adopt flexible work arrangements and leverage digital collaboration tools to maintain productivity and employee engagement. Implementing technologies that facilitate remote work fosters a culture of trust and autonomy, essential for attracting and retaining talent in today's job market. Furthermore, remote work can contribute to sustainability by reducing the carbon footprint associated with commuting and office space usage, aligning with the principles of sustainable business practices.

Finally, digital transformation must also prioritize diversity and inclusion initiatives. A diverse workforce brings varied perspectives, leading to more innovative solutions and better decision-making. By leveraging digital tools to create inclusive environments, businesses can ensure that all employees feel valued and empowered to contribute. This alignment not only enhances employee well-being and mental health but also strengthens the organization's ability to connect with a diverse customer base. As businesses embark on their digital transformation journeys, it is essential to integrate these values into their strategies, recognizing that a commitment to diversity and inclusion is integral to sustainable success in the future.

Tools and Technologies for Transformation

Tools and technologies play a crucial role in shaping the future of business, especially in an era where sustainability and innovation are paramount. As organizations strive to adapt to the changing landscape, they must leverage a variety of tools that enhance efficiency, promote sustainable practices, and improve overall performance. From digital platforms that facilitate remote work to advanced analytics that drive decision-making, the integration of these technologies can lead to transformative outcomes. Embracing these tools not only prepares businesses for the future but also aligns them with emerging consumer expectations regarding sustainability and corporate responsibility.

Digital transformation strategies are at the forefront of this technological evolution. Businesses are increasingly adopting cloud computing solutions, which offer unparalleled flexibility and scalability. These platforms enable teams to collaborate seamlessly, regardless of geographical barriers, thus supporting the rise of remote work innovations. Furthermore, automation tools are streamlining repetitive tasks, allowing employees to focus on more strategic initiatives. By embracing these digital solutions, organizations can enhance productivity while reducing their environmental footprint, as remote work often leads to decreased commuting and lower energy consumption in office spaces.

Artificial intelligence is another transformative technology that is reshaping business operations. AI-driven analytics provide insights into consumer behavior, enabling companies to tailor their offerings and improve customer experience. Machine learning algorithms can predict trends, optimize supply chains, and even enhance product development processes. Moreover, AI can support diversity and inclusion initiatives by mitigating biases in hiring and performance evaluations, fostering a more equitable workplace. As businesses harness AI's potential, they can drive innovation while ensuring that their practices align with the principles of social entrepreneurship and sustainability.

The circular economy model is gaining traction as companies seek to minimize waste and maximize resource efficiency. Tools designed for tracking materials and lifecycle assessments help organizations identify opportunities for reuse and recycling. Blockchain technology further enhances this model by providing transparency in supply chains, allowing businesses to trace the origins of materials and ensure ethical sourcing. This not only builds consumer trust but also encourages responsible consumption practices. By integrating circular economy principles into their operations, businesses can contribute to a more sustainable future while also realizing cost savings and operational efficiencies.

Finally, wellness and mental health in the workplace are becoming integral to modern business strategies. Technologies that support employee well-being, such as mental health apps and virtual counseling services, are gaining popularity as organizations recognize the importance of a healthy workforce. By prioritizing employee wellness, businesses can improve morale, reduce turnover, and enhance overall productivity. As the focus on employee experience grows, companies that invest in tools and technologies aimed at promoting mental health will not only attract top talent but also foster a culture of inclusivity and support. Together, these tools and technologies create a robust framework for businesses to innovate and thrive in a sustainable future.

Overcoming Barriers to Digital Change

Overcoming barriers to digital change is crucial for organizations aiming to thrive in the contemporary business landscape. Many companies encounter resistance due to entrenched mindsets, outdated technologies, and insufficient skills among employees. To navigate these challenges, it is essential to cultivate a culture that embraces continuous learning and adaptability. This involves fostering an environment where team members feel empowered to experiment with new tools and processes. By prioritizing education and support, businesses can alleviate fears associated with digital transformation and encourage a more innovative mindset.

The integration of digital technologies often faces hurdles related to infrastructure and resource allocation. Organizations must assess their current systems and identify gaps that hinder progress. Investing in robust technological frameworks and ensuring that employees have access to the necessary tools is critical for facilitating digital change. Moreover, leveraging external expertise can provide valuable insights and guidance, helping organizations to implement new technologies effectively. By adopting a strategic approach to resource management, companies can better position themselves to embrace digital transformation.

Resistance to change can also stem from a lack of clear communication regarding the benefits of digital initiatives. It is vital for leaders to articulate a compelling vision that highlights how digital transformation aligns with the organization's goals and values. Engaging employees in discussions about the potential impact of digital tools on their roles can demystify the process and foster buy-in. Transparency about the expected outcomes not only builds trust but also encourages collaboration among team members in embracing new practices.

Additionally, addressing the diverse needs of the workforce is essential in overcoming barriers to digital change. Organizations must recognize that not all employees will adapt to new technologies at the same pace. Implementing tailored training programs that cater to varying levels of digital literacy can facilitate smoother transitions. By providing support and resources to individuals who may struggle, businesses can create an inclusive environment that promotes collective growth and innovation.

Lastly, the role of leadership cannot be overstated in driving digital change. Leaders must exemplify the values of adaptability and openness to new ideas, setting the tone for the entire organization. By actively participating in digital initiatives and demonstrating their commitment to transformation, leaders can inspire others to follow suit. Emphasizing the importance of digital change not only enhances operational efficiency but also positions the organization as a forward-thinking entity ready to tackle the challenges of tomorrow. Through strategic leadership, clear communication, and a focus on inclusivity, businesses can successfully overcome barriers to digital change and pave the way for a sustainable future.

Chapter 4: Remote Work Innovations

The Shift to Remote Work: A New Normal

The shift to remote work has emerged as a defining feature of the modern business landscape, fundamentally altering how organizations operate and how employees experience their work. This transformation, accelerated by global events, has redefined traditional workplace dynamics and necessitated a reevaluation of strategies across various sectors. Companies are now tasked with adapting to this new normal while maintaining productivity, engagement, and a sense of community among their workforce. As businesses embrace remote work models, they must consider innovative methods to foster collaboration and leverage technology effectively.

One of the key benefits of remote work is the potential for increased flexibility, allowing employees to balance their professional and personal lives more effectively. This flexibility can lead to enhanced job satisfaction and overall well-being, which are critical components of sustainable business practices. Organizations that prioritize employee wellness and mental health are likely to see improved retention rates and productivity levels. By creating policies that support work-life balance, companies can cultivate a healthier work environment that aligns with the principles of social entrepreneurship and corporate responsibility.

Digital transformation strategies play a crucial role in the success of remote work initiatives. Organizations must invest in the right technologies to facilitate seamless communication and collaboration among remote teams. Tools such as video conferencing, project management software, and cloud-based platforms have become essential in maintaining workflow and connectivity. Furthermore, the integration of artificial intelligence into these technologies can streamline processes, enhance decision-making, and provide valuable insights into employee performance and engagement, ultimately driving efficiency and innovation.

As the remote work trend continues to evolve, businesses must also prioritize diversity and inclusion initiatives within their remote teams. The flexibility of remote work can attract a more diverse talent pool, as geographical barriers are diminished. Companies have the opportunity to create inclusive environments that reflect a variety of perspectives and experiences. By embracing this diversity, organizations can foster creativity and innovation, which are essential for navigating the complexities of the circular economy and developing sustainable business models.

Lastly, customer experience enhancement remains a critical focus for businesses adapting to remote work. With many employees working from home, understanding customer needs and preferences becomes even more important. Companies must leverage data analytics and blockchain applications to gain insights into customer behavior and preferences, enabling them to offer personalized experiences. By prioritizing customer-centric approaches and utilizing technology effectively, businesses can thrive in this new normal, ensuring long-term success and sustainability in an increasingly competitive marketplace.

Tools for Enhanced Remote Collaboration

In the evolving landscape of business, remote collaboration tools have become essential for fostering productivity and connection among teams spread across various locations. As organizations embrace the flexibility of remote work, understanding and effectively leveraging these tools can significantly enhance communication, streamline workflows, and improve overall team dynamics. The integration of digital platforms tailored for collaboration not only supports efficiency but also aligns with sustainable business practices by reducing the carbon footprint associated with traditional office environments.

One of the most critical tools in the realm of remote collaboration is project management software. Platforms such as Trello, Asana, and Monday.com enable teams to organize tasks, set deadlines, and track progress in real time, ensuring that everyone is on the same page. These tools promote transparency and accountability, which are vital for maintaining high levels of productivity in a remote setting. By visualizing workflows and assigning specific responsibilities, businesses can enhance their operational efficiency while fostering a culture of collaboration and inclusivity.

Communication tools also play a pivotal role in enhancing remote collaboration. Applications like Slack and Microsoft Teams facilitate instant messaging, video conferencing, and file sharing, allowing teams to communicate effectively regardless of geographical barriers. These platforms support asynchronous communication, enabling team members to contribute at times that suit their schedules, which is particularly beneficial for organizations that operate across multiple time zones. Furthermore, the integration of artificial intelligence within these tools can streamline processes, such as scheduling meetings and managing tasks, ultimately improving the user experience and enhancing productivity.

In addition to project management and communication tools, cloud storage solutions like Google Drive and Dropbox provide a secure and accessible environment for collaboration. These platforms enable teams to store, share, and collaboratively edit documents in real time, reducing the risk of miscommunication and version control issues. By adopting cloud technology, organizations can enhance their operational resilience, ensuring that team members can access essential resources from anywhere, thereby supporting the principles of a circular economy by minimizing the need for physical resources.

Finally, incorporating wellness and mental health tools into remote collaboration strategies is crucial for maintaining employee engagement and morale. Platforms that promote mental well-being, such as Headspace for Work or wellbeing check-in tools, can be integrated into the daily routines of remote teams. By prioritizing employee wellness, businesses not only demonstrate their commitment to social entrepreneurship and diversity initiatives but also create a supportive environment that fosters creativity and innovation. As organizations continue to adapt to the demands of remote work, investing in the right tools for collaboration will be essential for building sustainable and resilient teams in the future.

Cultivating Company Culture in Remote Settings

Cultivating a strong company culture in remote settings is essential for fostering engagement, productivity, and a sense of belonging among employees. As businesses increasingly adopt remote work models, leaders must rethink traditional approaches to culture-building. A successful remote culture hinges on clear communication, shared values, and intentional engagement strategies that bridge the physical distance. Emphasizing transparency and inclusivity in virtual interactions can help employees feel valued and connected to the organization's mission, ultimately enhancing retention and performance.

One fundamental aspect of nurturing company culture remotely is establishing a robust communication framework. Regular check-ins, virtual team meetings, and open channels for feedback are vital components of this framework. Utilizing various digital tools can facilitate seamless communication, making it easier for teams to collaborate and share ideas. Additionally, encouraging informal interactions, such as virtual coffee breaks or team-building activities, can help recreate the social aspects of office life. This intentional blending of work and socialization fosters relationships that strengthen the overall culture of the organization.

Shared values play a crucial role in defining company culture, especially in remote environments. Organizations should strive to articulate their core values clearly and ensure that every employee understands how they contribute to these ideals. Incorporating values into daily operations—including decision-making processes, hiring practices, and performance assessments—can create a cohesive culture where employees feel aligned with the company's goals. Recognizing and celebrating employee contributions that exemplify these values reinforces their importance and encourages a culture of appreciation.

Inclusivity is another key element in cultivating company culture remotely. Diverse teams bring unique perspectives and ideas that drive innovation, making it essential to prioritize diversity and inclusion initiatives. Organizations should actively seek to create diverse hiring practices and provide training to mitigate biases. Additionally, creating platforms for underrepresented voices to be heard can foster an environment where all employees feel empowered to share their insights. This commitment to inclusivity not only enhances the culture but also leads to better decision-making and problem-solving.

Finally, prioritizing wellness and mental health within remote work settings is critical to sustaining a positive company culture. Companies should offer resources and support systems that promote employee well-being, such as mental health days, counseling services, or wellness programs. Encouraging employees to maintain a healthy work-life balance and providing the flexibility to manage their schedules can reduce burnout and increase job satisfaction. When employees feel cared for and supported, they are more likely to engage meaningfully with their work and contribute positively to the company culture. By addressing the holistic well-being of employees, organizations can cultivate a thriving culture that adapts to the evolving landscape of remote work.

Chapter 5: Artificial Intelligence in Business

AI Applications Across Industries

AI applications are revolutionizing a multitude of industries, driving innovation and efficiency while reshaping traditional business models. Within the realm of healthcare, AI is being utilized to enhance patient care through predictive analytics, enabling medical professionals to identify potential health risks before they escalate. Machine learning algorithms analyze vast amounts of patient data to provide insights that inform personalized treatment plans. This not only improves health outcomes but also contributes to more sustainable healthcare practices by reducing unnecessary procedures and optimizing resource allocation.

In the manufacturing sector, AI is transforming production lines through automation and predictive maintenance. Smart factories leverage AI-driven robotics to streamline processes, reduce waste, and improve output quality. By utilizing data analytics, manufacturers can predict equipment failures before they occur, minimizing downtime and extending the lifespan of machinery. This approach aligns with circular economy models, where the focus is on sustainability and the efficient use of resources, thereby reducing the environmental impact of industrial operations.

Retail is another industry experiencing a significant transformation due to AI. Enhanced customer experience is achieved through personalized recommendations and targeted marketing strategies driven by AI algorithms. By analyzing consumer behavior and preferences, retailers can tailor their offerings, ultimately increasing customer satisfaction and loyalty. Additionally, AI's role in inventory management helps businesses optimize stock levels, reducing waste and ensuring that products are available when customers want them, which is essential in promoting sustainable business practices.

In the financial services industry, AI applications are streamlining operations and enhancing decision-making processes. Algorithms are capable of analyzing market trends and consumer data, enabling better risk assessment and fraud detection. This not only improves operational efficiency but also fosters trust and transparency in financial transactions, which are key components of social entrepreneurship. Furthermore, AI-driven solutions help in creating more inclusive financial products that cater to diverse populations, thus supporting diversity and inclusion initiatives within the sector.

Finally, the integration of AI in remote work settings is reshaping how organizations operate and engage with their employees. AI tools facilitate communication, collaboration, and productivity among remote teams, ensuring that companies can maintain high levels of performance regardless of location. Additionally, AI-driven wellness programs are being developed to monitor employee mental health and promote a healthy work-life balance. These innovations not only enhance employee well-being but also contribute to a more sustainable and resilient workforce, demonstrating the multifaceted benefits of AI across various industries.

Ethical Considerations in AI Deployment

In the rapidly evolving landscape of artificial intelligence, ethical considerations play a crucial role in shaping how these technologies are deployed within businesses. As organizations harness

AI to streamline operations and enhance decision-making, it becomes imperative to address the ethical implications that accompany these advancements. Transparency, accountability, and fairness are foundational principles that should guide the development and implementation of AI systems. Businesses must ensure that AI algorithms are understandable and that their decision-making processes do not perpetuate biases or discrimination, thereby fostering a more equitable workplace and market environment.

One significant ethical concern is the potential for bias in AI algorithms. These systems learn from historical data, which can reflect existing inequalities and prejudices. If not carefully managed, AI can inadvertently reinforce these biases, impacting hiring practices, customer interactions, and even product offerings. Organizations need to prioritize diversity in their data sets and involve cross-disciplinary teams in AI development to mitigate the risk of bias. By ensuring a variety of perspectives, businesses can create more inclusive AI solutions that better serve diverse customer bases and promote social equity.

Data privacy is another critical ethical consideration in AI deployment. As businesses increasingly rely on personal data to train AI systems, the need to protect user privacy becomes paramount. Organizations must comply with data protection regulations and implement robust security measures to safeguard sensitive information. Furthermore, transparency in how data is collected, stored, and utilized is essential to maintaining trust with customers and stakeholders. By prioritizing ethical data practices, businesses can not only adhere to legal requirements but also enhance their reputation and customer loyalty.

Additionally, the impact of AI on employment raises ethical questions that organizations must confront. While AI has the potential to increase efficiency and create new job opportunities, it can also lead to job displacement and workforce anxiety. Companies should approach AI integration with a commitment to workforce development, investing in training and reskilling programs to help employees adapt to new technologies. By fostering a culture of continuous learning and supporting employees through transitions, businesses can mitigate the negative consequences of automation and contribute to a more sustainable workforce.

Finally, the deployment of AI should align with broader social and environmental goals. Organizations have the opportunity to leverage AI for social good, addressing issues such as climate change, resource management, and public health. By incorporating ethical considerations into their AI strategies, businesses can drive innovation that not only enhances profitability but also contributes positively to society. In doing so, they position themselves as leaders in the new age of business, where ethical practices and sustainable growth are not just aspirations but fundamental components of success.

Future Trends in AI and Business

The future of artificial intelligence (AI) in business is poised to reshape industries and redefine the landscape of work. As organizations increasingly adopt AI technologies, they are discovering innovative ways to enhance efficiency, improve decision-making, and create personalized customer experiences. The integration of AI into various business processes allows for the automation of mundane tasks, freeing up human resources for more strategic endeavors. This transition not only boosts productivity but also fosters an environment where creativity and critical thinking can thrive, leading to a more dynamic workplace culture.

One significant trend is the rise of AI-driven analytics, which empowers businesses to make data-informed decisions. Advanced algorithms can analyze vast amounts of data to identify patterns and trends that may not be immediately apparent to human analysts. This capability is particularly beneficial in sectors such as retail and finance, where understanding consumer behavior and market dynamics is crucial. By leveraging AI analytics, companies can enhance their strategic planning, optimize their marketing efforts, and ultimately drive growth. As businesses become more data-centric, the demand for AI tools that can interpret real-time data will increase, enabling organizations to stay ahead of the competition.

Sustainable business practices are also being transformed through AI innovations. Companies are utilizing AI to develop more efficient supply chains, reduce waste, and minimize their carbon footprints. For example, AI can optimize logistics by analyzing routes and predicting delays, which helps in reducing fuel consumption and emissions. Furthermore, AI tools can assist in monitoring resource usage and identifying areas for improvement, thus promoting a circular economy model. As sustainability becomes a core component of corporate strategy, businesses that integrate AI into their sustainability initiatives will likely gain a competitive edge while fulfilling their social responsibility.

The landscape of remote work is another area where AI is making a significant impact. With the rise of hybrid work models, AI technologies are facilitating better collaboration and communication among teams. Virtual assistants, intelligent scheduling tools, and AI-powered project management systems are becoming essential for remote teams to function effectively. These tools not only streamline workflows but also enhance employee wellness by reducing the cognitive load associated with task management. As organizations continue to embrace remote work, the integration of AI into these frameworks will be crucial for maintaining team cohesion and productivity.

Finally, the future of AI in business will increasingly focus on ethical considerations, particularly concerning diversity and inclusion initiatives. As AI systems are developed, it is essential to ensure they are designed to be inclusive and free from bias. Businesses will need to prioritize responsible AI practices that promote equity and representation. By harnessing AI to analyze workplace demographics and employee feedback, organizations can identify gaps and implement strategies that foster a more inclusive culture. As social entrepreneurship gains traction, the alignment of AI development with ethical standards will be vital for building trust and ensuring that technology serves the greater good.

Chapter 6: Social Entrepreneurship

Defining Social Entrepreneurship

Social entrepreneurship is an approach to business that seeks to address social, cultural, or environmental issues while simultaneously generating profit. It operates at the intersection of commerce and social impact, where entrepreneurs leverage innovative strategies to create solutions that benefit society as a whole. Unlike traditional businesses that primarily focus on maximizing shareholder value, social enterprises prioritize creating positive change, often reinvesting profits back into their mission. This dual focus on social value and financial sustainability distinguishes social entrepreneurship from more conventional business models.

At the heart of social entrepreneurship lies the recognition that many of the world's pressing problems—such as poverty, inequality, and environmental degradation—cannot be solved through market forces alone. Social entrepreneurs take on the responsibility of addressing these challenges by developing sustainable business practices that promote social good. They often employ unique business strategies that aim to empower marginalized communities, enhance access to essential services, and promote sustainable development. The drive to innovate solutions to societal problems often leads social entrepreneurs to explore unconventional methods, including collaborations with non-profits, governments, and other stakeholders.

Digital transformation plays a significant role in the evolution of social entrepreneurship. With the rise of technology, social entrepreneurs can harness digital tools to scale their impact more effectively. For example, utilizing data analytics can help identify community needs more accurately, while e-commerce platforms allow for broader market reach. Additionally, social entrepreneurs can leverage social media to raise awareness of their causes and mobilize support, creating a community of advocates around their mission. This integration of technology not only enhances operational efficiency but also fosters greater transparency and accountability in their practices.

The principles of the circular economy further enhance the framework of social entrepreneurship by promoting resource efficiency and sustainability. Social enterprises often adopt circular economy models that focus on reducing waste and reusing materials, leading to more sustainable production and consumption patterns. By prioritizing these principles, social entrepreneurs can create innovative products and services that not only meet market needs but also contribute to environmental sustainability. This alignment with circular economy principles exemplifies how social entrepreneurship can lead to both economic and ecological benefits, ultimately paving the way for a more sustainable future.

As we navigate the complexities of tomorrow's business landscape, social entrepreneurship will continue to be a vital component in addressing global challenges. By defining success not just in financial terms but also through social impact, social entrepreneurs inspire a new generation of business leaders to think beyond traditional profit motives. Their commitment to fostering change through innovative strategies, sustainable practices, and collaborative efforts positions them as key players in the transition towards a more equitable and sustainable economy.

Models of Successful Social Enterprises

The landscape of social enterprises has evolved significantly, showcasing diverse models that prioritize not only profit but also social impact. Successful social enterprises often adopt hybrid structures that blend traditional business practices with social mission-driven initiatives. These models can vary widely, from non-profit organizations that generate revenue through social businesses to for-profit enterprises that reinvest profits into community projects. By embracing flexibility and innovation, these enterprises demonstrate that financial sustainability and social responsibility can coexist, paving the way for a more equitable economic model.

One prominent model of a successful social enterprise is the "B Corporation," which certifies companies that meet rigorous standards of social and environmental performance, accountability, and transparency. B Corps, such as Patagonia and Ben & Jerry's, illustrate how businesses can operate with a dual mission: to generate profit while positively impacting society and the environment. This model encourages enterprises to adopt sustainable practices, fostering a culture of responsibility that resonates with consumers increasingly concerned about corporate ethics. As a result, B Corps often enjoy enhanced brand loyalty and customer engagement, proving that ethical practices can lead to commercial success.

Another compelling model is the "social franchise," which replicates the business model of a successful social enterprise in different locations while maintaining the core mission. Brands like Grameen Bank and TOMS Shoes have effectively utilized this model to expand their reach and impact. By empowering local entrepreneurs through training and resources, social franchises create jobs, stimulate local economies, and promote social change. This approach not only amplifies the social mission but also ensures that the enterprise remains adaptable to the unique needs of local communities, fostering a sense of ownership and engagement among stakeholders.

The "cooperative model" is also gaining traction as a viable framework for social enterprises. Cooperatives are owned and operated by their members, allowing for democratic decision-making and profit-sharing. This model promotes equity and inclusion, as seen in successful cooperatives like Equal Exchange and the Mondragon Corporation. By prioritizing member welfare over profit maximization, cooperatives can address social issues while achieving financial viability. Additionally, this structure empowers individuals and communities, enhancing their capacity for self-determination and contributing to a more just and sustainable economy.

Lastly, the "impact investment" model exemplifies how social enterprises can attract funding while emphasizing social returns. Impact investors seek to generate measurable social and environmental benefits alongside financial returns, driving capital towards businesses that prioritize positive change. Companies like Warby Parker and Beyond Meat have leveraged this model to scale their operations and amplify their social missions. As more investors recognize the value of sustainable practices, the impact investment model is becoming increasingly influential in shaping the future of business, encouraging innovation and collaboration within the social enterprise sector. Together, these diverse models illustrate the multifaceted nature of successful social enterprises and their potential to drive meaningful change in tomorrow's economy.

Measuring Social Impact

Measuring social impact is a critical component of modern business practices, particularly as organizations strive to align their operations with sustainable and ethical objectives. Social impact refers to the effect that an organization's activities have on its community and environment, encompassing economic, social, and environmental dimensions. As businesses increasingly adopt frameworks for social responsibility, the need for effective measurement tools becomes paramount. Various methodologies exist, ranging from qualitative assessments to quantitative metrics, allowing businesses to gauge their contributions to society and the environment.

One of the most widely recognized frameworks for measuring social impact is the Social Return on Investment (SROI) model. This approach quantifies social, environmental, and economic outcomes, translating them into monetary values. By applying SROI, businesses can assess the return generated from investments in social initiatives, helping to demonstrate the financial viability of social entrepreneurship. Furthermore, SROI encourages transparency and accountability, enabling stakeholders to understand the true impact of an organization's activities and investment in community welfare.

Another method for measuring social impact involves the use of Key Performance Indicators (KPIs) tailored to specific sustainability goals. KPIs can be customized to reflect the unique mission and values of an organization, focusing on areas such as diversity and inclusion, employee wellness, or environmental sustainability. For instance, a company might track metrics related to employee engagement, retention rates, or carbon footprint reductions. By establishing clear KPIs, businesses can not only enhance their operational effectiveness but also communicate their social impact to customers and stakeholders, reinforcing their commitment to social responsibility.

In an era where digital transformation is reshaping business practices, technology plays a significant role in measuring social impact. Advanced data analytics and blockchain technology can provide real-time insights into an organization's social initiatives. By leveraging these tools, companies can track progress, identify areas for improvement, and ensure that their efforts align with their stated goals. Moreover, digital platforms can facilitate stakeholder engagement, allowing businesses to gather feedback and insights from the communities they serve, fostering a more inclusive approach to social impact measurement.

Ultimately, measuring social impact is not just a compliance exercise; it is an opportunity for businesses to innovate and differentiate themselves in a competitive landscape. As consumers increasingly prioritize social responsibility in their purchasing decisions, organizations that effectively measure and communicate their social impact can enhance customer loyalty and brand reputation. By embracing measurement as a core aspect of their strategy, businesses can contribute to a sustainable future while simultaneously driving profitability and fostering a positive societal impact.

Chapter 7: Circular Economy Models

Understanding the Circular Economy

The circular economy presents a transformative approach to economic growth that prioritizes sustainability and resource efficiency. Unlike the traditional linear model, which follows a "take-make-dispose" pattern, the circular economy emphasizes the continuous use of resources, aiming to minimize waste and maximize value. This model encourages businesses to rethink product design, manufacturing processes, and lifecycle management, ensuring that materials are reused, repaired, refurbished, and recycled. By adopting circular principles, organizations can reduce their environmental impact while also creating new economic opportunities.

At the core of the circular economy is the concept of resource optimization. This involves designing products that are not only durable and easy to repair but also versatile enough to serve multiple purposes throughout their lifecycle. For instance, companies are increasingly exploring modular designs that allow for easy upgrades and repairs, ultimately extending the lifespan of products. This shift not only reduces waste but also fosters innovation, as businesses are challenged to develop new materials and processes that align with circular principles. By focusing on resource efficiency, organizations can significantly lower their production costs and enhance their competitive advantage.

Digital technologies play a crucial role in the implementation of circular economy models. The rise of the Internet of Things (IoT), artificial intelligence, and blockchain technology enables businesses to track and manage resources more effectively. IoT devices can monitor product usage and performance, allowing companies to offer maintenance services that extend the lifecycle of their products. Meanwhile, blockchain can enhance transparency in supply chains, ensuring that materials are sourced sustainably and reused appropriately. These digital transformation strategies not only facilitate the transition to a circular economy but also provide organizations with valuable data insights that inform decision-making and optimize operations.

Social entrepreneurship is another vital component of the circular economy, as it seeks to address societal challenges through innovative business practices. By prioritizing sustainability and community well-being, social enterprises can drive systemic change while also achieving financial viability. These organizations often focus on creating circular solutions that not only benefit the environment but also empower local communities. By engaging in partnerships with stakeholders, including governments and non-profits, social entrepreneurs can leverage collective resources to foster sustainable practices that align with circular economy principles.

Incorporating the circular economy into business models also enhances customer experience and promotes diversity and inclusion initiatives. As consumers become increasingly aware of environmental issues, they are more likely to support businesses that prioritize sustainability. Companies that adopt circular practices can differentiate themselves by offering products and services that resonate with eco-conscious consumers. Furthermore, by engaging diverse teams in the design and implementation of circular solutions, businesses can benefit from a wide range of perspectives and ideas, fostering innovation and resilience in an ever-evolving marketplace. Embracing the circular economy is not just a trend; it represents a fundamental shift in how businesses operate and interact with their stakeholders, paving the way for a sustainable future.

Benefits of Circular Practices

The adoption of circular practices presents numerous benefits that extend beyond environmental sustainability. At the core of these practices is the idea of designing systems that retain value within the economy for as long as possible, reducing waste and resource consumption. Companies that embrace circularity can expect to see a significant reduction in operational costs. By reusing materials and optimizing resource flows, businesses can minimize their reliance on virgin resources, leading to lower procurement costs and less exposure to fluctuating raw material prices. This financial advantage is particularly vital in today's volatile market conditions, where sustainability is increasingly intertwined with economic resilience.

In addition to cost savings, circular practices can enhance a company's brand reputation and customer loyalty. As consumers become more environmentally conscious, they seek out businesses that demonstrate a commitment to sustainability. By adopting circular economy models, companies can position themselves as leaders in sustainable innovation, appealing to a growing demographic that prioritizes ethical consumption. This enhanced brand image not only attracts new customers but also fosters loyalty among existing ones, ultimately translating into increased market share and profitability.

Moreover, implementing circular practices can stimulate innovation within organizations. The transition from a linear to a circular model encourages businesses to rethink product design, materials used, and overall operational processes. This shift can lead to the development of new products and services that are not only eco-friendly but also more efficient and cost-effective. Through collaboration and knowledge sharing, businesses can leverage digital transformation strategies and artificial intelligence to identify opportunities for innovation that may not have been apparent within traditional linear frameworks.

Circular practices also contribute to social entrepreneurship and community well-being. By focusing on sustainable practices, businesses can create job opportunities in new sectors related to recycling, refurbishing, and resource management. This not only supports local economies but also promotes diversity and inclusion initiatives by engaging underrepresented communities in the green economy. The holistic approach of circularity ensures that social equity is considered alongside environmental health, fostering a more inclusive and sustainable future for all.

Finally, the integration of circular economy principles can significantly enhance customer experience. As companies shift toward offering services rather than products, they can foster deeper relationships with customers through subscriptions, sharing platforms, and take-back schemes. This not only provides customers with greater value but also encourages responsible consumption habits. By aligning business models with the principles of circularity, companies can create a more engaged and loyal customer base, paving the way for a sustainable future that benefits both businesses and society at large.

Case Studies of Circular Economy Success

The concept of the circular economy has gained traction as businesses seek innovative ways to promote sustainability while also achieving economic growth. Case studies from various industries illustrate how organizations have successfully implemented circular economy principles, transforming waste into valuable resources. One prominent example is the fashion industry, where companies like Patagonia have pioneered initiatives to encourage customers to repair, reuse, and recycle their products. By adopting a model that emphasizes durability and responsible consumption, Patagonia not only reduces the environmental impact of its operations but also fosters a loyal customer base that values sustainability.

In the realm of technology, companies such as Dell have embraced circular economy practices by designing products for longevity and recyclability. Dell's closed-loop recycling program allows the company to reclaim materials from old devices and use them in new products, significantly reducing the need for virgin materials. This approach not only minimizes waste but also lowers production costs and enhances the company's reputation as a leader in sustainable practices. By integrating circularity into their product lifecycle, Dell demonstrates that innovation can align with environmental stewardship.

The construction industry presents another compelling case study with the rise of modular building techniques. Companies like Katerra are revolutionizing the traditional construction model by utilizing prefabrication and sustainable materials, which reduce waste and energy consumption. Their approach enables buildings to be easily disassembled and repurposed at the end of their lifecycle, promoting resource efficiency and minimizing environmental impact. This case illustrates how integrating circular economy principles can lead to more efficient, sustainable, and economically viable building practices that meet the demands of modern society.

In the food sector, organizations such as Loop Industries are making strides in creating a circular economy by transforming waste into valuable products. Loop focuses on recycling plastics that would otherwise end up in landfills, turning them back into high-quality materials for use in new products. Their innovative approach not only addresses the plastic waste crisis but also demonstrates the potential for a thriving market built on circular principles. This case study highlights how industries can leverage technology and creativity to develop sustainable solutions that benefit both the economy and the environment.

Lastly, social enterprises like Warby Parker exemplify the intersection of circular economy and social responsibility. By implementing a buy-one, give-one model, Warby Parker ensures that for every pair of glasses sold, another is distributed to someone in need. This initiative not only addresses the issue of accessibility in eyewear but also promotes a culture of reuse and sustainability. Warby Parker's success showcases how businesses can thrive while making a positive social impact, reinforcing the idea that a circular economy fosters innovation that benefits society as a whole. These case studies collectively illustrate that the transition to a circular economy is not only feasible but also presents opportunities for diverse industries to innovate, engage with customers, and contribute to a sustainable future.

Chapter 8: Blockchain Applications for Enterprises

Introduction to Blockchain Technology

Blockchain technology has emerged as a transformative force in the business landscape, offering innovative solutions that align with the principles of transparency, security, and decentralization. At its core, blockchain is a distributed ledger system that allows for the secure and transparent recording of transactions across multiple computers. This technology ensures that once a transaction is recorded, it cannot be altered retroactively without altering all subsequent blocks, thereby providing an inherent level of trust and integrity. As businesses increasingly seek to enhance their operations and foster sustainability, understanding the fundamentals of blockchain becomes crucial.

One of the most compelling aspects of blockchain is its ability to facilitate secure peer-to-peer transactions without the need for intermediaries. This feature is particularly valuable in the realm of digital transformation strategies, where companies are looking to streamline processes and reduce costs. By eliminating middlemen, businesses can not only save money but also minimize the time it takes to complete transactions. This efficiency is especially beneficial for remote work innovations, where teams require reliable and rapid access to information and resources, enabling them to collaborate effectively regardless of their physical locations.

In addition to its efficiency, blockchain technology promotes sustainability through its capacity to enhance supply chain transparency. By providing a traceable record of a product's journey from production to consumption, blockchain enables companies to verify ethical sourcing and ensure compliance with sustainability standards. This is particularly significant for social entrepreneurship and circular economy models, where accountability and ethical practices are paramount. Companies can demonstrate their commitment to sustainability by leveraging blockchain to provide consumers with verifiable information about the products they purchase, fostering a deeper connection between businesses and their customers.

The applications of blockchain extend beyond transactions and supply chains; they also encompass areas such as wellness and mental health in the workplace. For instance, organizations can utilize blockchain to securely store employee health data while giving individuals greater control over their own information. This not only enhances privacy but also fosters a culture of trust and openness within the workplace. Furthermore, the transparency of blockchain can help in creating more diverse and inclusive environments by ensuring equitable access to opportunities and resources, thereby supporting initiatives that promote diversity.

As businesses navigate the complexities of the modern landscape, the integration of blockchain technology offers a pathway to innovation and resilience. By understanding its principles and applications, organizations can harness the power of blockchain to enhance customer experience, streamline operations, and promote sustainable practices. In an era defined by rapid change and digital transformation, blockchain stands out as a critical tool that can help shape the future of business, aligning with the values and expectations of a new generation of consumers and stakeholders.

Use Cases in Various Industries

The adoption of innovative practices across industries is reshaping the landscape of business and contributing to a more sustainable future. Various sectors are harnessing the power of technology and new business models to address pressing challenges while enhancing operational efficiency. For instance, in the manufacturing sector, the integration of circular economy principles is becoming increasingly prevalent. Companies are redesigning their supply chains to minimize waste, utilizing recyclable materials, and implementing take-back schemes to repurpose products. This approach not only reduces environmental impact but also appeals to eco-conscious consumers, proving that sustainability can drive profitability.

In the realm of healthcare, the application of artificial intelligence is transforming patient care and administrative processes. AI-driven tools are streamlining diagnostics, predicting patient outcomes, and personalizing treatment plans. Telemedicine, further accelerated by remote work innovations, enables healthcare providers to reach patients in underserved areas, ensuring equitable access to services. This digital transformation not only enhances the patient experience but also contributes to operational efficiency, allowing healthcare professionals to focus more on patient care rather than administrative burdens.

The retail industry is also witnessing significant shifts as businesses leverage blockchain technology to enhance transparency and trust with consumers. By tracking the provenance of products and ensuring ethical sourcing, retailers can build stronger relationships with customers who prioritize sustainability. This technology enables businesses to provide verifiable claims about their products, fostering an environment of accountability and encouraging responsible consumer behavior. Additionally, customer experience enhancement is achieved through personalized shopping experiences driven by data analytics, allowing retailers to cater to individual preferences and needs.

Social entrepreneurship is gaining momentum across various sectors, where businesses are focused on addressing social issues while maintaining profitability. Organizations are developing innovative solutions to tackle problems such as poverty, education, and access to clean water. By blending social impact with business objectives, these enterprises not only contribute to community well-being but also create new markets and opportunities for collaboration. This approach exemplifies the potential of business to serve as a catalyst for positive change, aligning profit motives with societal benefits.

Finally, the emphasis on diversity and inclusion initiatives is reshaping workplace culture across industries. Companies are recognizing that diverse teams foster creativity and innovation, leading to better problem-solving and decision-making. By implementing comprehensive training programs and creating inclusive environments, organizations can empower all employees to contribute their unique perspectives. Additionally, prioritizing wellness and mental health in the workplace is essential for retaining talent and maintaining productivity. As businesses embrace these strategies, they not only enhance their internal culture but also position themselves as leaders in the evolving business landscape, committed to a sustainable and equitable future.

Future of Blockchain in Business

The future of blockchain in business is poised to transform various sectors by enhancing transparency, security, and efficiency. As organizations increasingly recognize the potential of this decentralized technology, they are exploring its applications beyond cryptocurrency. Blockchain can streamline operations, reduce fraud, and enhance trust in transactions, making it an invaluable tool in the modern business landscape. With businesses adopting a digital-first approach, the integration of blockchain into traditional practices promises to redefine how companies operate and interact with stakeholders.

One of the most promising applications of blockchain technology is in supply chain management. By providing an immutable ledger that tracks goods from origin to consumer, businesses can enhance traceability and accountability. This transparency not only helps in verifying the authenticity of products but also enables companies to respond swiftly to issues such as recalls or disputes. As consumers increasingly demand sustainable and ethically sourced products, blockchain offers a solution to verify compliance with environmental and social standards, thereby supporting sustainable business practices.

In the realm of financial transactions, blockchain has the potential to revolutionize payment systems and banking processes. Traditional banking methods often involve intermediaries that slow down transactions and increase costs. Blockchain's decentralized nature allows for peer-to-peer transactions, reducing fees and accelerating processing times. Furthermore, smart contracts can automate and enforce agreements without the need for intermediaries, minimizing human error and enhancing efficiency. As businesses look for ways to adopt digital transformation strategies, blockchain provides an innovative solution that aligns with the need for speed and reduced operational costs.

Moreover, blockchain can significantly enhance customer experience by offering secure and personalized interactions. With increasing concerns over data privacy, consumers are becoming more cautious about sharing their information. Blockchain empowers customers by allowing them to control their data through decentralized identities, fostering trust and confidence in transactions. This shift not only enhances customer loyalty but also enables businesses to tailor their offerings based on verified customer preferences, driving engagement and satisfaction.

As organizations move towards more sustainable and inclusive practices, blockchain technology can facilitate social entrepreneurship efforts and promote diversity and inclusion initiatives. By providing a platform for transparent fundraising and resource allocation, blockchain can empower marginalized communities and support innovative business models that prioritize social impact. Additionally, its ability to create secure digital identities can help individuals in underserved areas access financial services and opportunities. As the business landscape evolves, embracing blockchain will be crucial for companies aiming to innovate responsibly and create lasting value in a rapidly changing world.

Chapter 9: Wellness and Mental Health in the Workplace

Importance of Employee Well-Being

Employee well-being has emerged as a critical component of modern business strategy, especially in the context of evolving workplace dynamics and the increasing demands of a rapidly changing economy. Organizations that prioritize the health and happiness of their employees are not only fostering a positive work environment but also paving the way for enhanced productivity and innovation. In a landscape where talent acquisition and retention are paramount, businesses that invest in well-being initiatives demonstrate a commitment to their workforce, which translates into a competitive edge in the market.

The integration of well-being into business practices promotes a culture of engagement and loyalty among employees. When individuals feel supported—both mentally and physically—they are more likely to contribute positively to their teams and the organization as a whole. This sense of belonging can lead to lower turnover rates, reduced absenteeism, and a stronger organizational identity. As remote work continues to redefine traditional employment structures, companies that adapt their well-being strategies to accommodate flexible work arrangements will likely see increased employee satisfaction and performance.

Mental health, in particular, has gained significant attention in recent years, with organizations recognizing its direct link to overall employee productivity and organizational success. By fostering an environment where mental health is openly discussed and supported, businesses can mitigate the stigma often associated with mental health challenges. Initiatives such as employee assistance programs, wellness workshops, and mental health days are becoming essential components of comprehensive well-being strategies. These programs not only benefit employees but also enhance the company's reputation as a socially responsible entity.

Moreover, the intersection of technology and well-being cannot be overlooked, especially as businesses embrace digital transformation. Tools such as wellness apps, virtual counseling services, and AI-driven health assessments are revolutionizing how organizations approach employee health. By leveraging technology, businesses can offer personalized wellness solutions that cater to the unique needs of their workforce. This innovation not only improves accessibility but also allows for a more data-driven approach to assessing the effectiveness of well-being initiatives.

Ultimately, prioritizing employee well-being is not merely a trend but a sustainable business practice that aligns with the broader goals of social entrepreneurship and corporate responsibility. As organizations increasingly recognize the importance of compassion and support within their cultures, they are likely to foster a more diverse and inclusive workforce. This holistic approach to employee well-being not only benefits individuals but also enhances customer experience and drives long-term business success in an ever-evolving marketplace.

Strategies for Promoting Mental Health

Promoting mental health in the workplace is essential for fostering an environment where employees can thrive and contribute to the organization's success. In the New Age of Business, where innovation and adaptability are key, companies must prioritize mental health strategies that align with sustainable business practices. This includes creating a culture that values open communication and encourages employees to discuss their mental health challenges without fear of stigma. By implementing regular mental health check-ins and providing resources such as counseling services or mental health days, organizations can demonstrate their commitment to employee well-being.

Digital transformation strategies play a critical role in promoting mental health by leveraging technology to connect employees and create a supportive environment. Utilizing digital platforms for virtual team-building activities can help strengthen relationships among remote workers, reducing feelings of isolation. Additionally, businesses can invest in mental health apps that offer mindfulness exercises, stress management techniques, and access to mental health professionals, making support accessible anytime and anywhere. The integration of technology in promoting mental health not only enhances employee experience but also aligns with the overall goal of fostering a resilient workforce.

Remote work innovations have reshaped the traditional work environment, necessitating a new approach to mental health support. Organizations should consider flexible work schedules that allow employees to balance their professional and personal lives effectively. Providing training for managers on recognizing signs of mental distress and how to support their teams can create a more empathetic workplace culture. Furthermore, encouraging regular breaks and the establishment of boundaries between work and home life are vital strategies that can help employees manage their mental health while working remotely.

Artificial intelligence in business can be harnessed to enhance mental health initiatives by analyzing employee feedback and identifying patterns in workplace stressors. AI tools can help organizations tailor their mental health programs to meet the specific needs of their workforce. By analyzing data trends, companies can proactively address issues before they escalate, creating a more supportive environment. This data-driven approach not only improves employee well-being but also contributes to the overall productivity and success of the organization.

Social entrepreneurship and diversity and inclusion initiatives are integral to promoting mental health as they foster a sense of belonging among employees from diverse backgrounds. Companies that prioritize inclusivity create an environment where everyone feels valued and supported. Encouraging employee resource groups and mental health ambassador programs can provide platforms for sharing experiences and resources, enhancing community and support within the organization. By embedding these principles into their core operations, businesses can create a sustainable culture that champions mental health, ultimately leading to a more engaged and productive workforce.

Measuring the Impact of Wellness Programs

Measuring the impact of wellness programs is an essential aspect of understanding their effectiveness within modern organizations. As businesses increasingly prioritize employee well-being, it becomes crucial to establish metrics that accurately reflect the outcomes of these initiatives. Organizations can utilize a variety of quantitative and qualitative measures to assess the impact of wellness programs, including employee engagement scores, absenteeism rates, productivity levels, and overall job satisfaction. Collecting and analyzing this data allows organizations to evaluate the return on investment of their wellness initiatives and make informed decisions about future enhancements.

One effective method for measuring the impact of wellness programs is through employee surveys and feedback mechanisms. By regularly gathering input from employees, organizations can gain insights into how wellness programs are perceived and utilized. Surveys can evaluate the specific aspects of wellness offerings—such as mental health resources, physical fitness activities, and work-life balance initiatives—and assess their effectiveness in meeting employee needs. This qualitative feedback can be instrumental in identifying areas for improvement and tailoring programs to better serve the workforce, ultimately fostering a culture of well-being.

In addition to employee feedback, organizations can track observable metrics that indicate the overall health of their workplace environment. Monitoring absenteeism rates can provide insight into the effectiveness of wellness programs, as reduced absenteeism often correlates with improved employee health and satisfaction. Similarly, tracking productivity metrics before and after the implementation of wellness initiatives can highlight their impact on performance. By correlating wellness program participation with these key performance indicators, organizations can establish a clearer understanding of the tangible benefits associated with their investments in employee well-being.

Furthermore, integrating technology into wellness program assessments can enhance data collection and analysis. Digital tools, such as health apps and wearable devices, can provide real-time data on employee activity levels, stress management, and overall health metrics. These insights can be aggregated and analyzed to identify trends and patterns, enabling organizations to make data-driven decisions about program adjustments. Leveraging artificial intelligence in this context can also facilitate predictive analytics, helping businesses anticipate the evolving needs of their workforce and adapt wellness offerings accordingly.

Ultimately, measuring the impact of wellness programs is not just about assessing immediate outcomes; it also involves understanding the long-term benefits to both employees and the organization as a whole. A comprehensive evaluation of wellness initiatives can reveal their influence on employee retention, engagement, and overall organizational culture. By committing to ongoing assessment and improvement of wellness programs, businesses can ensure they are not only enhancing employee well-being but also cultivating a sustainable and productive workplace that aligns with the broader goals of innovation and social responsibility in the future of business.

Chapter 10: Customer Experience Enhancement

Understanding Customer Experience

Understanding customer experience is essential for any business aiming to thrive in the rapidly evolving landscape of tomorrow. At its core, customer experience encompasses all interactions a customer has with a brand, from the initial point of contact through post-purchase support. This holistic view highlights the importance of every touchpoint in shaping perceptions and fostering loyalty. In the age of digital transformation, businesses must recognize that customers expect seamless, personalized interactions that cater to their specific needs and preferences.

One of the key drivers of exceptional customer experience is the integration of technology. Artificial intelligence plays a significant role in analyzing customer data, allowing businesses to anticipate needs and tailor their offerings accordingly. By leveraging AI, companies can create predictive models that enhance personalization, making customers feel valued and understood. This technological advancement not only improves satisfaction but also builds a deeper emotional connection between the brand and its customers, which is crucial in today's competitive marketplace.

Furthermore, sustainable business practices are increasingly becoming a focal point for customers. Consumers today are more environmentally conscious and socially aware than ever before. They seek brands that align with their values, contributing to a demand for transparency and ethical practices. Businesses that prioritize sustainability in their operations are likely to enhance their customer experience by fostering trust and loyalty. By communicating their commitment to sustainable practices, companies can create a compelling narrative that resonates with their audience, encouraging long-term relationships.

In addition to sustainability, diversity and inclusion initiatives are integral to enhancing customer experience. A diverse workforce brings a variety of perspectives that can lead to more innovative solutions and products tailored to a broader audience. When customers see themselves represented in a brand's messaging and offerings, it reinforces a sense of belonging and connection. This inclusivity not only improves customer satisfaction but also drives brand loyalty, as consumers increasingly prefer to support companies that reflect their values.

Lastly, understanding customer experience is not a one-time effort but an ongoing process that requires continuous feedback and adaptation. Businesses must implement strategies for gathering customer insights and utilize them to refine their approaches. In the realm of remote work, this means ensuring that employees are equipped and empowered to deliver exceptional service, even from a distance. By fostering a culture of wellness and mental health in the workplace, companies can enhance employee engagement and, in turn, improve the overall customer experience. By prioritizing these facets, businesses can position themselves for success in an ever-changing environment, ultimately shaping a sustainable future.

Tools for Enhancing Customer Interactions

In the evolving landscape of business, enhancing customer interactions has become essential for building loyalty and fostering sustainable growth. The integration of advanced tools and technologies plays a pivotal role in this endeavor. Companies can leverage customer relationship management (CRM) systems to streamline communication, gather insights, and personalize engagements with their customers. These systems not only help in tracking customer interactions but also enable businesses to analyze data patterns, leading to more informed decision-making and tailored marketing strategies that resonate with diverse customer bases.

Artificial intelligence (AI) is another transformative tool that can significantly enhance customer interactions. AI-powered chatbots and virtual assistants can provide immediate responses to customer inquiries, ensuring that support is available around the clock. These technologies not only improve response times but also free up human resources to focus on more complex customer needs. By utilizing AI to analyze customer feedback and behavior, businesses can gain deeper insights into customer preferences and pain points, allowing for more proactive and meaningful engagements that align with customer expectations.

Digital platforms have also revolutionized the way businesses interact with their customers. Social media, for example, offers a dynamic space for brands to connect directly with their consumers. By actively engaging on these platforms, companies can build communities, gather real-time feedback, and showcase their commitment to sustainability and social responsibility. This two-way communication fosters trust and transparency, essential elements for modern consumers who prioritize ethical practices and corporate accountability.

In the context of remote work innovations, collaboration tools such as video conferencing and project management applications facilitate seamless communication between teams and customers. These tools enable businesses to maintain a high level of service quality, regardless of geographical barriers. Remote work technologies also allow for greater flexibility, making it easier for companies to adapt to changing customer needs and preferences, which is crucial in today's fast-paced environment. By embracing such tools, organizations can ensure that customer interactions remain positive and productive, even when teams are dispersed.

Lastly, incorporating wellness and mental health initiatives into customer interaction strategies can significantly enhance the overall customer experience. By prioritizing employee well-being, companies can create a more engaged and motivated workforce, which translates to better service for customers. Training staff to handle customer interactions with empathy and understanding ensures that clients feel valued and heard. Furthermore, promoting diversity and inclusion within teams can lead to a broader range of perspectives, enhancing creativity and problem-solving in customer engagement strategies. This holistic approach not only benefits the customer but also cultivates a sustainable business model that aligns with the values of today's consumers.

The Future of Customer Engagement

The landscape of customer engagement is evolving rapidly, driven by technological advancements and shifting consumer expectations. As businesses navigate this new terrain, they must adopt innovative strategies that prioritize customer experience and foster meaningful connections. In this context, the future of customer engagement will be characterized by personalization, transparency, and inclusivity, allowing organizations to resonate more deeply with diverse audiences. Embracing these elements will not only enhance customer loyalty but also position businesses as leaders in sustainable practices and social responsibility.

Digital transformation strategies are at the forefront of this evolution, enabling organizations to harness data and analytics for deeper insights into customer behavior. By leveraging artificial intelligence, companies can create tailored experiences that anticipate customer needs and preferences. This proactive approach enhances customer satisfaction and encourages ongoing engagement. Additionally, the integration of blockchain technology can provide transparency in transactions, building trust and confidence among consumers. As businesses adopt these technologies, they must remain mindful of ethical considerations, ensuring data privacy and security while fostering an open dialogue with customers.

Remote work innovations also play a crucial role in shaping future customer engagement. As teams adapt to flexible work environments, businesses can leverage digital tools to maintain strong connections with customers. Virtual interactions can be enhanced through immersive technologies, such as augmented and virtual reality, creating unique experiences that go beyond traditional customer service. Moreover, remote work fosters a diverse workforce capable of understanding and addressing the needs of varied customer demographics. This diversity can lead to more inclusive marketing strategies and product offerings that reflect the values and preferences of a broader audience.

Social entrepreneurship and wellness initiatives are increasingly influencing customer engagement strategies as consumers seek brands that align with their values. Businesses that prioritize social impact and employee well-being are more likely to attract and retain customers who prioritize sustainability and ethical practices. This shift toward purpose-driven engagement not only enhances brand loyalty but also contributes to a positive workplace culture. Companies that invest in the mental health and wellness of their employees are better positioned to deliver exceptional customer experiences, as satisfied employees tend to drive customer satisfaction.

Looking ahead, organizations must also consider the implications of the circular economy in their customer engagement strategies. By promoting sustainable practices and encouraging responsible consumption, businesses can engage customers in meaningful ways that resonate with their values. This may involve developing products designed for longevity, repairability, and recyclability, thereby fostering a sense of community among environmentally conscious consumers. In this future landscape, customer engagement will be defined not only by transactions but by the shared commitment to sustainability and ethical practices, paving the way for a more inclusive and responsible business environment.

Chapter 11: Diversity and Inclusion Initiatives

The Business Case for Diversity

The business case for diversity is more compelling than ever, especially in the rapidly evolving landscape of modern enterprises. Diverse teams bring a variety of perspectives that foster creativity and innovation, essential components for businesses aiming to thrive in the New Age of Business. Research shows that companies with diverse workforces are 35% more likely to outperform their competitors in terms of profitability. This is largely due to the enhanced problem-solving abilities that diverse teams possess, allowing them to approach challenges from multiple angles and devise more effective solutions.

Moreover, diversity is not just a moral imperative; it is a strategic advantage that aligns closely with sustainable business practices. As organizations increasingly prioritize environmental, social, and governance (ESG) criteria, a diverse workforce can better understand and address the needs of different stakeholders, including customers, employees, and the communities they serve. A company that embraces diversity is more likely to innovate in its sustainable practices, creating products and services that resonate with a broader audience, ultimately driving customer loyalty and brand reputation.

In the context of digital transformation strategies, diversity plays a critical role as businesses leverage new technologies to enhance their operations. A diverse team is adept at utilizing various digital tools and platforms to address unique market challenges and customer needs. This adaptability is particularly crucial as organizations navigate the complexities of remote work innovations and the increasing reliance on artificial intelligence. Diverse teams can identify biases in AI algorithms and ensure that the technology is developed and deployed in a manner that is inclusive and equitable, preventing potential pitfalls that could arise from a homogenous perspective.

Social entrepreneurship and circular economy models also benefit from the integration of diverse viewpoints. A diverse workforce is better positioned to identify social challenges and devise solutions that are not only economically viable but also socially responsible. This approach not only contributes to community development but also aligns with the principles of sustainability, creating a positive feedback loop that enhances the overall impact of business initiatives. By prioritizing diversity, organizations can ensure that their business models are resilient and adaptable, capable of responding to both market demands and societal needs.

Finally, the focus on wellness and mental health in the workplace highlights the importance of diversity in creating an inclusive environment where all employees feel valued. Organizations that prioritize diversity and inclusion initiatives are more likely to cultivate a workplace culture that promotes psychological safety, allowing employees to express their ideas and concerns freely. This not only enhances employee engagement and satisfaction but also leads to better customer experience enhancement. Ultimately, the business case for diversity is not merely about compliance or filling quotas; it is about embracing a holistic approach that drives innovation, resilience, and long-term success in tomorrow's business landscape.

Implementing Effective Inclusion Strategies

Implementing effective inclusion strategies is essential for businesses seeking to thrive in an increasingly diverse and interconnected world. At the core of these strategies lies the recognition that every individual, regardless of their background or perspective, contributes unique insights that can drive innovation and enhance problem-solving. Organizations that prioritize inclusivity are better positioned to attract and retain top talent, improve employee morale, and foster a culture of collaboration. This chapter explores various inclusion strategies that can be integrated into business practices to create an environment where everyone feels valued and empowered.

One of the most impactful inclusion strategies involves the establishment of clear policies and practices that promote diversity in hiring and promotion processes. This can be achieved by implementing blind recruitment techniques, ensuring diverse interview panels, and setting measurable diversity goals. By focusing on skills and potential rather than traditional credentials, businesses can tap into a wider talent pool, including individuals from underrepresented backgrounds. Additionally, organizations should regularly assess their hiring practices to identify and eliminate biases that may hinder inclusivity.

Training and development programs play a critical role in fostering an inclusive workplace. These programs should be designed to educate employees about the importance of diversity and inclusion, equipping them with the tools to recognize and address unconscious biases. Furthermore, creating mentorship opportunities that connect employees from diverse backgrounds with seasoned professionals can enhance career development and build a strong sense of belonging. By investing in the growth of all employees, organizations can cultivate a culture of respect and understanding that drives engagement and productivity.

Incorporating employee feedback into decision-making processes is another effective inclusion strategy. Businesses can establish forums or regular surveys to gather insights on employees' experiences and perceptions of inclusivity within the organization. By actively listening to their workforce, companies can identify areas for improvement and implement changes that reflect the needs and preferences of their employees. This approach not only empowers individuals but also fosters a sense of ownership and accountability across the organization, reinforcing the importance of inclusivity in achieving common goals.

Finally, leveraging technology can enhance inclusion efforts significantly. Digital tools and platforms can facilitate remote work, allowing organizations to tap into a global workforce and accommodate diverse working styles. Artificial intelligence can be utilized to analyze workplace dynamics and provide insights into employee engagement and satisfaction. By integrating these technological advancements, businesses can create a more flexible and inclusive work environment that aligns with the evolving needs of their employees. Emphasizing inclusion is not just a moral imperative; it is a strategic advantage that can propel businesses toward sustainable success in the future.

Measuring the Success of D&I Efforts

Measuring the success of diversity and inclusion (D&I) efforts is critical for organizations striving to cultivate an equitable workplace. The first step in this process involves establishing clear, quantifiable goals that align with the overall mission of the business. Organizations should define what success looks like, whether through increasing representation in leadership roles, improving employee engagement scores, or enhancing overall workplace culture. By setting specific benchmarks, companies can create a framework for evaluating their D&I initiatives and ensure that these efforts are meaningfully integrated into all aspects of the organization.

Data collection plays a pivotal role in assessing the effectiveness of D&I strategies. Organizations should utilize both qualitative and quantitative methods to gather insights on employee experiences and perceptions. Surveys, focus groups, and interviews can provide valuable information about the inclusivity of workplace culture and the impact of D&I programs. Furthermore, analyzing demographic data can help identify areas where disparities exist, allowing organizations to target their efforts more effectively. By employing a comprehensive approach to data collection, businesses can gain a clearer picture of their D&I landscape and track progress over time.

Another essential aspect of measuring D&I success is the regular evaluation of initiatives and policies. This involves not only assessing outcomes but also understanding the processes that lead to those outcomes. Organizations should implement ongoing reviews of their D&I programs to determine what is working and what needs adjustment. This iterative approach encourages a culture of continuous improvement, where feedback is actively sought and incorporated into future strategies. By fostering an environment of adaptability, businesses can respond more effectively to the evolving needs of their workforce.

Leadership accountability is key to sustaining D&I efforts. Organizations should establish mechanisms for holding leaders responsible for D&I outcomes, such as tying performance metrics and incentives to diversity goals. When leaders are visibly committed to D&I and understand their role in fostering an inclusive environment, it sends a powerful message throughout the organization. This accountability can also extend to all employees, encouraging a collective commitment to inclusivity that transcends the top levels of management.

Finally, it is crucial for organizations to communicate their D&I successes and challenges transparently. Sharing progress reports with employees, stakeholders, and the broader community not only highlights commitment but also fosters trust and engagement. Transparency allows for an open dialogue about the journey toward inclusivity, enabling organizations to celebrate achievements while acknowledging areas that require further effort. In doing so, businesses can cultivate a sense of shared responsibility and collective action, which is vital for sustaining the momentum of D&I initiatives in the long term.

www.ingramcontent.com/pod-product-compliance
Lightning Source LLC
Chambersburg PA
CBHW081021240526

45471CB00018B/3933